THE SERVANT:

CORRECTING A FLAWED DESIGN

COPYRIGHT © 2022, DONALD S. DAY

"This book is dedicated to my amazing friends, my wonderful family and my beautiful wife. In equal parts this book is dedicated to all my athletes I've ever have or currently do serve. You all are the engine behind the machine, and I love each and every one of you dearly."

- Donald S. Day

"Remember your why, think about your why."

- Lonnie Brown

Why the upside-down pyramid?

Traditional Leadership Style   Servant Leadership

Leader   Leader

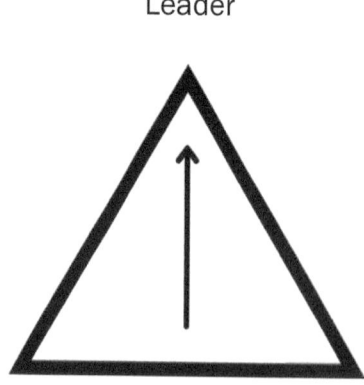
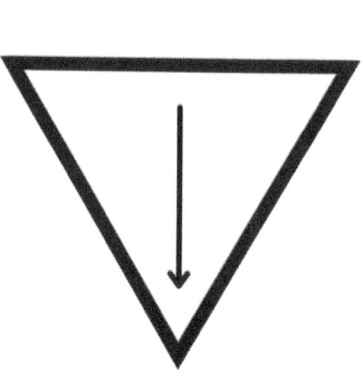

Followers   Followers

On the left-hand side is the traditional style of leadership we have been told about and seen throughout history. In this style of leadership, the burden is on the follower to pour everything into the leader. While on the right-hand side we see the type of leadership that will be discussed within the contents of this book. This is the servanthood style of leadership where the leader pours everything he has into his followers. Strap up and enjoy the ride.

Table of Contents

Prologue: Self Actualization

Who am I? I guess a better question would be who are you? You know who I am, I'm the guy who wrote the book that you are now reading. Knowing who I am does absolutely nothing for you, accept provide some sort of validity into what you're going to read in the next few chapters. Regardless of this off-beat fact though knowing who I am, in the grander scheme of things, will not help you achieve whatever you are looking for within the pages of this book. Sure, you may gain valuable information whether or not you do know who you are. But that information will come and go the same way knowing what the temperature of the day is with no long-lasting impact or dramatic changes made to the life that you are "living". So before we waste my time and yours let's dive into who exactly you are but more so how to figure that out.

If you are looking for a self-help book then alas I am afraid you've come to the wrong place. This book will not give you self-help as you alone are the only person capable of helping yourself. This book is quite the contrary in its purpose. I wrote this book for you to help others. For one cannot fill a cup if they are pouring from an empty cup and today's version of leadership that's been glamorized is a perfect metaphor for the empty filling cup. But we will get into that later. For now, let's talk about the most important part of leadership and that is knowing thyself.

What do I know about myself? Who am I? Why am I the person who has the capacity or validity to write a book on servanthood or leadership? I mean, I've been a good leader and a terrible one. By no means am I perfect or someone whose name will be mentioned with the MLK's of the history books. I'm an ordinary person just like yourself. On the day I was born the clouds did not part from the skies and I have never led any type of army into battle. So what grandiose thought-provoking knowledge could I have to shed from the standpoint of being an average joe like the rest of humanity...I have sacrificed for my people, time and time again.

I am in a semi-exclusive industry in the sports performance world and have done it for some time. I've been fortunate enough to train some high-level athletes and make some very good connections. I have spoken at national conferences and won championships in multiple sports. I've been a director multiple times since I was in my mid-twenties. I've worked at the top schools "quote-unquote" in my field and have founded my own DEI company. I've also spent years writing numerous articles for a very well-known company. I've taken on the giants of the industry and battled winning and losing battles. I've transformed many athletic departments and also ruined relationships in the process. But that is all that I've done, none of that is who I am.

There are many people who do not know the distinction between the two. Who you have little to do with what you've done. There are some connections between the two as behaviors no doubt ably elicit actions but there is still a clear-cut difference between the two. Most people want to see themselves in a positive light. Even the people that think negatively of themselves want sympathy which in turn...puts themselves back into a positive light. This is why it is important to know that what you have done and who you are for the contexts of this book are completely different things.

I am a husband. I am a guy who takes big risks and will gamble the house whether I am up big or down big. I am a dreamer in the most hopeless romantic sense of the word. I am a lifelong learner in part to the fact that I make a lot of mistakes. I have a deep-rooted pride that sometimes gets the best of me that causes careless actions and egotistical mistakes. I am a natural leader but a piss poor manager though I have improved with meticulous efforts put into getting better. I am a different person to different groups of people, this is a fact I know but do not care about because I am a person who cares very little about a lot of things. Though I do care very much about a few things. This is helpful while sometimes hurtful to my progress through my walk-in life. I am a person who must follow a strict set of codes to stay on track because

I do not have the self-discipline to be skillfully undisciplined. I am not a liar nor am I someone who wants to see others harmed. And I will lose everything for what I believe in.

Do you notice the difference in the who I am vs what I've done paragraphs? What you've done paints a picture that is most times beautiful. Who you are reveals the truth. Most of what I've done (good and bad) has been a pinpoint correlation of who I am. Now I don't have mastery in zen. I've had to realize who I am by facing some hard truths, asking the right people, and spending time with myself. At the time of this writing, I'm almost thirty-one years old. It has taken decades for me to come to grips with who I am. I've put the work into figuring out who I am due to one reason and one reason alone…I cannot be an effective leader if I don't know who the person leading is. If I don't know myself, how can I expect to believe that I'm making the right decisions for the team vs personal gain? If I don't know myself, how can I ever be effective at learning how someone else ticks? How could I ever have the heart of a servant if I don't know if my heart is even in the right place?

These sound like silly questions, but I've made decisions before that I thought were in the best interest of those around me only to find out years later these decisions were that of a selfish child. My lens was cloudy, and I did not have the foresight to clean it. I would make brash, rash, emotional decisions without having a guiding set of codes by which to live but I asked others to trust my decisions. Were they all bad? No, we saw tremendous growth in our department my first time as a leader. But I damaged some relationships that did not need to be so and at the end of the day, I knew I could do better. Usually when things are going well and you still think you can do better…there's something to that.

I was twenty-six or so and had recently become the director of my department. At this age, I was the youngest director in the country working division one football sports performance. Our team had been abysmal years prior. In this year we went on to become bowl eligible (something no one had thought we could do). On top of being young and feeling on top of the world, it was also the first time I was making money (close to six figures). But I knew I could be better. I knew I didn't have it all figured out. I also knew my pride was ruling my world and I did not like who I was becoming. It's easy to say I got pissed off and found another job. But the truth of the matter was I needed to go learn and become better than I was going to be had I stayed in the route I was headed. The first of my many steps of learning who I was. So I left, took a 50% pay cut, traveled from New York to BFE Georgia, and became an assistant again, eager to learn something more about myself.

Georgia was a tremendous three years of growth for me. I was continuously metaphorically beaten to a pulp and had to force myself to get back up. I struggled with my job, I struggled with the second Civil Rights movement, I struggled in marriage, I struggled as a leader, and just about every other aspect of life you can think of. I was constantly forced to grow tougher after each loss and rebuild after every victory. And victory never lasted long nor did they occur often. It was a great renaissance of sorts within growth as a man, my time spent down in Georgia. Everyone believes they know what they stand for (who they are) but in the moments of sacrifice many people realize who they are and who they wish they were are two different people. At that point in my life, I realized who I was and who I wanted to be were not that far off. I stood up against oppression, and I made many great sacrifices. I sacrificed my job standing up to an authority figure I deemed as hateful and oppressive. This does not make me a hero, it makes me a person and it was a test in a long series of trials.

I truly was blessed to be able to live out these moments. At the time were they hard? Yes. But I was not going to sit silent or still in the face of oppression so much so that at times I put a target on my own back. This was who I am, not what I had done. Again, I point out and use these examples to drive home a point so many people miss out on. Who you are has nothing to do with what you have done. I know people who have spoken at female clinics that have been hailed to high merit in my industry, who also took part in my proverbial lynching. But how could someone of that esteem do something so cruel? Because who they are has nothing to do with what they have done. Who you are is the person you see when you dive deep into the mirror, the person who you think of when you lay down at night and reflect on yourself, something most people don't do.

Self-actualization is not a glamorous thing. I do not carry around a self-actualized badge of honor to show off to my cousins at family re-unions. Nor do I particularly enjoy being aware of who it is that I am. It is a constant fight to be at peace with every single negative aspect, every single weakness, and every single downfall. This in itself though is the reward that self-actualization does bring. There is peaceful chaos to it. When you know exactly who you are and have conversations with those who do not know who they are, you realize their ignorance. Their blind loyalty to protecting their fragile ego perhaps or perhaps the extreme fear that causes them to hide even from themselves.

The remedy for blindness is the removal of ego, self-interest, and fear. Ego is a fire that burns and warps anything in its path. Self-interest is the sugar that can make anything you snack on taste good but is slowly killing you as you eat it. And fear is in itself nothing but the fabrication of lies that you have chosen to believe. Fear is doubt, and doubt is a fable built in one's head. Any of the three will ruin your path to self-actualization ironi-cally though most actualization happens after at least one of these terrible traits are conquered for these traits are holding the door to self-actualiza-tion shut for many people. I have let almost all three hold me back at one time or another both knowingly and unknowingly at times.

We have already discussed ego, being the youngest director in the nation making more money than I could spend, so let's talk about fear. Many people are afraid of who they really are. And this fear makes them doubt if people would like them if they knew who they really were. That fear lets them build a façade or a wall for people either to see something they are not or to block the parts they deem less favorable to others. Fear in a way can be tied in with self-interests to a certain extreme dependent on the person's fears. I believe most fear is embedded in self-interest due to humans naturally having a selfish nature to them. To be a servant is not normal for most people which we will discuss in later chapters. But first, we will continue our journey through self-actualization.

There was once a man who would tell me everything I was doing wrong and very bluntly. I had asked him to do this. I wanted to make sure I was working on my blind spots. This man seemed to be working his as well, but I was getting the sense I was being judged more than helped after an extended amount of time. It does not feel good to hear your blind spots constantly, but I also wanted to make sure my pride wasn't hurting my progress. So, we continued. This went on for almost a year while this man worked for me. We would do a lot of self-actualization "training" while drinking bourbon and sharing cigars and talking about life, sharing ideas on leadership and business.

This man, who holds himself in the highest regard as a leader, would eventually leave to start his career path in a different field. He would always joke that even though he worked technically for me he would always go on to tell people later on that he worked with me, not for me. This joke always rubbed me the wrong way. He would also say things like he has sat where I sat before though he had not quite sat where I had. The comparison would be a very shrewd one at best. He would also watch from a safe distance as I endured my fights in Georgia, not hurting but also doing nothing to help. He would also go on to take my business ideas for himself and turn a profit. This is still a man who holds himself in the highest regards as a leader, in fact, runs the leadership business that we had often talked about over drinks at his house.

Of course, if you asked this man about this story, he would tell a slightly different account as I'm sure anyone in that situation would. And by that, I do not mean the situation of someone "caught doing wrong" I'm talking about someone who is not self-actualized due to fear. Fear of one's self-interest. When someone paints a picture and believes it to be true of who they are it is due to fear. When someone steals their image from someone else and truly believes it belongs to them, it is deep-rooted insecurity and fear that are blocking them from being able to self-actualize. I did not start my Ph.D. because I wanted to, I did that because this man inspired me to. This man is no self-actualized Gandhi, he is the Einstein who took the theories from the other clerk. And that is okay too because business is dirty and ruthless. But what is not okay is to fall into a trap of believing you are someone you are not.

No one is perfect, I have done some shady things throughout my life that most would say make me a bad person. These are things I have come to terms with throughout my journey. There are many shady businessmen that you have to think twice about before entering business deals with. But they know exactly what they are about to do to whoever they decide to trick because they know exactly who they are and so should you. Self-actualization isn't all about the silver linings. There is no way you will be able to be "unblemished". There are going to have to be flaws that you are okay with because you realize what they are and how they make you who you are. I enjoy drinking, and at times I can drink too much. But I will always love drinking as I have my entire life. I hurt nobody by drinking and I do not drink often enough to hurt myself. Would some say that my drinking is something I should slow down on or cut out? I am sure it is. But for me, it is a pool I choose to wade in.

There is nothing glamorous about that statement nor does that necessarily feel good to say, but it is who I am. It is also something I have under control and don't let get out of hand because I have accepted who I am and the lengths to where I can go. In college, I could not drink sociably or have a glass of bourbon with my cigar. Now I can simply sit back and enjoy a nice glass by the pool or in my hot tub on the weekends. When I was younger, I would go out with the other coaches on away trips, as I've gotten older it's gotten to the point, I know myself, so I choose to just watch tv quietly in my hotel room instead of going out on the town.

Do these things make me sound bad? Of course, they do. But I use them to illustrate a point of how vital it is to know who you are because if you know the animal, you will know what it is capable of.

There will be a lot of facts in this book used to illustrate points. The best way history can be told is through the sharing of facts throughout generations. I won't use names to illustrate my facts because there is a lack of self-actualization. I on the other hand know who I am and will freely talk about myself throughout this book as well to drive home some other points that need to be made throughout this book. You cannot run away from who you are. And I will choose never to do so.

My way of leading may not be for everybody and that's okay. I merely want to give you a better shot of success at leading than I was given. I had read tons of "self-help" books disguised as leaderships books. But these books were flawed in their leadership models. Now as I learn what leadership truly is I want to share it with the world which is why I wrote this book. I am no JK Rowling, so I do not expect to be on 60 Minutes discussing the contents of this book but if one person takes this book and learns from it then I have done my job. Some men make one disciple while others make thousands. Whatever my capacity is, I will rest on that.

Part 1: The Flawed Leadership Model

Just yesterday (or whenever yesterday is when this book is published) I was watching a man whom I work with not doing anything while the rest of us cleaned the weight room up. We had just gotten done with a lift group and needed to hurry and clean so we could rush over to practice. Now, this is nothing new, this man very rarely ever helped set up or clean. The reason I watched this particular day is that it was food for thought for me.

This man-made double of what I made even though he had about half of my experience. He also did about one-fifth of the work that I did in my current role. Just a few days prior it was brought to my attention that my boss's boss had begun the conversation about this co-worker's lack of effort. I assumed that he would be fired at some point in time and maybe at the time of this reading he is. But in that brief moment of observation, I realized something completely wrong with leadership that I had known but forgotten. The flawed design of what leadership is.

You see this co-worker of mine was given the tasks of being the meta-physical or spiritual or some type of gatherer of the team. The tradi-tion bought by my boss from another school was on Thursdays (two days before game day) we played a highlight video in the weight room and gave a message to the team. I very rarely stayed to listen not be-cause of the fact I did not agree with this tradition but because I did not like who was delivering the message, my lazy co-worker who could do nothing right.

To say I did not like this man may be misspoken, I cannot listen to someone speak of things they do not live out in their everyday life or at least try to. I identify myself as a follower of Christ but my lifestyle doesn't always align with that message. But I know that following in Christ's footsteps is not about perfection, it is about dependence. And

I've always thought there's beauty in that. That our dependence in itself is a direct reflection of our flaws as humans. That we are never expected to be perfected in a sense of God has a soft spot for us within this fact of our moral ambiguity. But regardless of this he still extends his open arms to us. I by no means try to be the guru of Christianity because within my self-actualization I know I have a strong dependence on God because I am blind in my walk and need my handheld so my footsteps may follow behind his. But it's through this acknowledgment that I can guide others with similar struggles as mine.

I live a lifestyle of the constant need for dependence. If I were God or Christ, then maybe I could hold people to judgment but I am neither so I chose not to judge others or pretend to know God's will as I don't even truly know God. IF I did claim to know God's will without even truly knowing the depths of who God is...then I would be a hypocrite. And that is why I never stayed to listen to my lazy ex co-workers' Thursday messages. He would in his mind consider himself a leader of men, a beacon of sorts if you let him tell it. If you asked him about servanthood and sacrifice, there is no doubt in my mind he would give personal examples of both. Unfortunately, without any self-actualization, he would be telling you meaningless nothings as his behaviors do not produce the actions of servanthood.

He's not the only leader who does this. Many leaders lead based on the "George Washington Model". This is the model based on the picture of George Washington crossing the Delaware River with his hand on his hat, standing proud in the front of the boat. If there was a light coming from the sky that light would be shining brightly upon him. But the only thing that is moving the boat is the people around him. No light shining down on their blood, sweat, and tears and no recognition of their hard work. They are mindlessly taking a command given to them by their egocentric leader and continuing to "row the boat". This is the type of leadership leaders seem to feed on nowadays. Where the commander is the guy who has "made it" or "paid his dues" (regardless of if true or not) but does not feel the need to do much outside of managing his subordinates. This type of model is that everyone has a job model and the higher up you are it seems as if your job is to do the least amount of work to reap the maximum number of benefits.

And in today's capitalistic market who wouldn't agree with the thought process of that model. Making the most by doing the least is pretty much how America was founded on the backs of others doing the most and making the less. So why change this model? Why would you do anything other than keep the top fat and the bottom level management hungry? The top is where the most important people sit and the ones at the bottom can be easily replaced right? No, not so much.

How many times have you gone to work and thought "my boss is an idiot how did he get this job" or thought to yourself "the only reason my boss has this job is because of (insert cliché but normalized scenario)". Now, how many times have you sat back and thought to yourself..."man my boss is the type of guy who would do anything for us, he's a true leader" well unless you're very lucky I bet not too many times. In this chapter, we're going to break down not only why you have had the bosses you have but why traditionally your bosses haven't been leaders. As we even talk about eventually what corruptions will deplete the servanthood of a leader as well.

We'll first start with the problem before we give the solution. We've talked a lot already about what modern leadership looks like and why it resides in our society. The main reason for the modern form of leadership is because it's easy and selfish. I believe it's important for you to know what I mean by the "modern form" of leadership. We can all agree there are many different eras of time and for the purpose of this book there will be constant references to two eras: the modern era and the historic era.

I defy the modern era as the current era we live in dating back to the times after Christ. The historic era was everything from the days of Christ's last walk on Earth to the times before that. I don't want you to think I'm going to force-feed Christianity down your throat but servanthood is a direct reference to a biblical model of leadership there for there will be many references made to Christ's leadership philosophies that I have taken to mold my thought process behind leadership.

This has nothing to do with your belief system or your spiritual preferences just as a discussion on the history of toilets is not a personal belief system debate on your devotedness behind the creator of toilets, simply a discussion that brings upon a better understanding of how he made this toilet. I say all that to say this, read this book with an open mind because there are much deeper rabbit holes we will go down outside of a Christ-inspired leadership model. Trust me (insert ambiguous evil cartoonish laugh to myself).

I have a habit of getting off track and going down a spiral of metaphors and stories. In conversations, it can be annoying for the listener, but I think in book form it helps add to the content of the book. Now time to retrace our path back to my original starting point. The reason that most of you haven't had a transcendent boss is that your boss is like every other boss you've ever had. Though some of them may be great managers, management and leadership are not the same. You do not need to be a great leader to be a great manager and in the business world, you can get away with being a mediocre leader but a phenomenal manager. And on the other token, you can be a great leader but have poor management skills.

I have been called a great leader in different instances, but I know that my management skills are very subpar. The only reason I have ever been able to produce unprecedented change within different companies is because of my servant-style leadership (which we will expand on in later chapters). Most hiring managers within a corporation do not care to inspire others through their hires but rather, as a point of emphasis, want to increase their bottom line. It's more about production than it is about the people. Especially in the business world.

Now in my world of athletics...it's about production more than it is about the people. Though my world is inhabited by hundreds of hundreds of former athletes (whether high school or college or even professional) that originally got into sports because they were inspired by the leadership of some coach, they were either personally coached by or that they have seen on television. So, though I do not believe hiring managers care that much more in sports than business how good of a leader you are as long as the bottom line gets taken care of, leadership does have a great deal of respect in my world. You would be amazed how many times I've heard "yeah he's not a great x's and o's guy at all but he's a phenomenal leader". But the drawback to that in my field is there are also a lot of unqualified people put into leadership roles that do not belong there.

What I mean by that is that having a lot of former athletes (some professional) in leadership positions means that there are a lot of people who just have jobs because of what they did as athletes or maybe they are famous alumni of the school they're working at. They have never been leaders nor managers so how can they be expected to do either. Just as in the business world just looking at the bottom dollar and ignoring those who get that dollar to rise is not a wise decision neither is hiring someone just based on who they are and not what they've done. In either case, all that is happening is that the wrong type of person is being propelled into leadership roles.

Now sometimes a corporation gets lucky and hires a transformational leader on accident or they saw something in him that blossomed with the opportunity to lead. But more often than not they just hired another person. This is why your bosses have sucked because they are just doing what everyone else does. Copy and paste from a flawed system of leadership. The system was designed to glorify one and subjectify the others therefore it will never lead to the followers feeling like more than cheese pieces that can be sacrificed at any time. But if the system is that bad then why do people do it? It's lazy, easy, and glorifies the leader. That is why.

Digging deeper into the flaws of the George Washington leadership model. The people are the ones who matter. But in this leadership model, the people do not matter. The people are replaceable as they are just cogs in the machine and not necessarily the machine itself. When the only thing that matters is the leader then it doesn't matter who the people underneath him are. Even if the bottom line starts to suffer it's on the leader to sacrifice the pawns to desperately find a way to turn things around.

In football the first thing to go is not the head coach, it's the offensive coordinator, the defensive coordinator, or the strength staff. Usually, the head football coach is the last person to go. Even though he is the one who hired these people and put them in the position to hurt the production of the team. The problem most of the time is the leader, so sacrificing the people is only a stall for more time and hopeful desperation that the team clicks enough to keep the leader around just a little longer. Very rarely do you find sustained success in college football. Most of the time you find replications of success for minimal amounts of time. The Bobby Bowden's of the world are unfortunately no longer here.

In corporations where the people feel like ants there is not much deep-rooted trust built inside the building. I used to have a boss whom I did not like at first. In fact, I despised this man. I was interning upstairs with the football staff and when they told me a position downstairs in the weight room had opened that would be a paid opportunity for, I said I'd never go down there. I'd rather work for free than work for someone I despised that much. Eventually though I was talked into going down and working that position.

The first few days were not as bad as I had over-dramatized them to be in my head prior. He treated us all as equals and he did a great job of including all of us in everything (for the most part). He had some rookie mistakes but don't we all. He did much better as a leader at 23 than I had done at the age of 26 when I had a chance to lead a football team and staff for the first time. On Fridays he would always bring each member of the staff into the offices and have one on one meetings about where we stood, what we were doing good and what we needed to improve on. He would do this while we cleaned the entire weight room, plucking us away momentarily one by one. Then when he was done with those meetings he would come out and clean the weight room with us. This exact gesture of servanthood is what cemented him as our leader in our eyes.

Back then I didn't appreciate it as much as I do now, smiling fondly while writing these past events down. At the time I believed that every boss should be doing those exact same things. I believed that it made sense that people would do exactly what he did and the fact he helped us clean a weight room we all worked in did not make him some messiah figure but a normal person. Much later on in life, I would realize that what he was doing was not a normal occurrence. I've had bosses in their 40's and bosses in the middle to late '20s since then and not many of them have ever gone to the length of servanthood that my 23-year-old boss had back in the day.

It took me many years as both an assistant and as a director to find out what I wanted in life. Hopefully, at the time of this publication, I've only had nine coaching jobs (which is still a lot). I have worked the highest levels of college athletics, I've won championships/bowl games / legendary games. I have done a lot but I have been a journeyman most of my career. Right now I believe I'm entering my eleventh year as a coach and have been at nine different schools. One of those schools I was at for three years, the other school two years, and the rest of the schools have been within a six-year window. I've moved from New York to Georgia to Arizona and right back to the east coast in the way of Kentucky. That all happened within five years.

The reason I "job hopped" so much at the beginning was that I wanted to keep moving forward in my career. Then I had my come to Jesus moment in New York that brought me to Georgia where I spent three years. In Georgia, I had found an answer to a question I had often asked myself: what's going to make me happy at a job? This question was answered to me in a different barrage of ways. I enjoy the freedom and not being micromanaged or controlled. I also enjoy leading due to the fact I truly believe so many people (myself included at times) miss the boat on what leadership is. You can't make someone a better leader, only life and time does that. But you can make yourself a better leader. But the biggest takeaway from Georgia I found out was that servant leadership is a model I needed to follow. It was what I learned all those years ago with my 23-year-old boss and it was not a common thing. Finding a servant leader is very uncommon amongst most corporations.

There's a saying that people like to be told what to do or controlled or ruled or whatever due to it's comforting. And for some people that might be true. They might like to fit themselves into a little box and try to feel secure inside their very structured walls. But I believe most people more so than being ruled, seek to be served. There is comfort and security in service. When you are being served you know that someone is taking care of you and putting you first above themselves.

If you've ever worked in the food industry you would know this to be true. I was a dishwasher for many years at a local chain restaurant and in doing that I learn the true meaning of the service industry. I would wash dishes for hours on end before I could eat. And if the dishes got backed up while I was on break, I had to quickly run to make sure the dishes were getting done enough for me to sit back down and eat. Now by no means was I a Gandhi, going on a hunger strike to bring about peace, but damnit it's my book and my metaphors!

The people who ate in the restaurant never thanked me for my role as a dishwasher and also a part-time busboy. They didn't know my name, nor did they know one detail about my own life. I got no tips from them, and my work wasn't widely recognized or publicized in the local newspaper. I did what I did because it was my job and because it was my assigned duty to do my role in making sure the people were being served properly. And little did I know this would be my first step towards being a servant leader. Also, during this time, I had my first major heartbreak when a hostess dumped me and then proceeded to date a cook so multiple life lessons were learned during this period of my life.

When I moved to Arizona from Georgia, I did not expect to find the same abundance of servant leaders that I had in Georgia. But I did find one. He was my direct boss but he was the associate director which made him above me on the sliding scale so I respected him the same way I would a boss. It had been almost a ten-year gap since the last time I had worked for a servant leader (with some exceptions here and there) and it was refreshing that I worked with a man like this. This particular job was grueling. In my industry, most people throw around the word "grind" or "hard work" whatever it may be. This is to either justify to some phantom audience how hard they work or other reasons unbeknownst to me. I say this because we all work tough hours. Twelve-hour days are normal and nine-hour days are short. Even on days off, most of the time we are in the office because if you're not seen you're forgotten. But this job in Arizona was not a grind...it was one of the most grueling experiences of my life.

I often joked with the associate director that I enjoyed not having a job better than I did working. Or that when the next Civil Rights movement happens, I'm going to sit on the sideline and let someone else put their careers at risk. Now that's a joke but it is not an understatement to say one of the most grueling times in my life was going through the Civil Rights movement that I had just previously gone through before the first seven months of my time in Arizona. My time in Arizona was part of the journey. And it brought the associate director into my life's path.

This man was the definition of a servant leader in all aspects of life. He always had done anything he could to help anyone out and he was just genuinely a good person. He would take my wife and me out to dinner, he would pay for things when we were all together and he almost electrocuted himself helping me wire my hot tub. And he also took part in all of those grueling experiences during our time together in Arizona. A few times that I can think of specifically were the experiences with setting up lifts and set up of the fieldwork sessions.

I want to preface this before I dive into these two scenarios that I am not bashing anyone. I am going to just list two examples to serve as how the associate director was a servant leader. This doesn't make anyone less of or make him more of these are just two experiences I had with him. I enjoyed my time in Arizona and it led to a lot of positive financial things for me later on in life due to buying a house at a great time and reselling it at a better one. I also got to do a lot of stuff that I would take on with me later in my career in terms of training quarterbacks. I train my quarterbacks in the same manner that I train pitchers with little differences, but most things are interchangeable. But I was able to grow and hone my skill set with baseball players by working with the quarterbacks in a very hands-off fashion from my boss for which I am very thankful.

Now back to the gruel. Our setup was more than I had ever seen or been accustomed to at previous jobs for both our normal lifts and for our fieldwork. If there was a piece of equipment in the room, it seemed that we found a way to use it. That led to a lot of positive increases in the key performance indicators that we tracked in the weight room but also killed our staff from physicality and difficulty of setting up standpoint. Full circle moment, the lazy co-worker that I had mentioned early on worked at this school with us. Back to our story.

There would be times when we would have to transport hundreds of pounds of chains around the field, hundreds of pounds of weighted sleds, etc. just for our set up for the workout. And on top of that, we would sometimes end up moving these chains, sleds, or whatever around like madmen during the workouts as the kids would get done using them. After each workout either on the field or in the weight room, the strength staff would have to clean up after the athletes. The athletes very rarely cleaned up any of their own weights. Which for me was something I was not used to (as you'll learn later in later chapters). Eventually, we did get this changed where athletes had to take after their own messes, but this wasn't until my last week of work before I moved on to another job. Thankfully I got to enjoy one week of the athletes setting things up themselves but for almost my entirety of work, I did not get this luxury.

The way our staff was set up our head guy did a lot of computer work with the other assistant and then me and the associate did most of the grunt work. Depending on the time of the year we had help, or we didn't for the first few months January until summertime we had no one to help us. We would show up an hour and a half early to set everything up and get things done for the setup. This, I promise you, is not normal but it's what we had to do. Now normally a whole staff would set up together or we would have interns to help set up (which we did later) but at first, it was just me and the highest-ranking assistant on staff who was our associate director.

He did not need to or have to help lead the setup as he did. In fact, he didn't have to do a lot of the stuff he did but he did it anyway. I used to tell him to do less that he was going to run himself ragged but I think part of what made him who he was is the fact that giving that much to others energized him. He would work technique work with the players after practice something that is usually reserved for the football coaches themselves, but the kids would come to our associate director and he wasn't going to turn them away. He would be walking around with a bum hip and bad back and teeth ready to fall out of his mouth but still help me lug around chains or set up our multi-processed lift. I can't sit here and say he didn't complain but we all complained in a way if we needed to release the stress and tension of the tasks that were expected of us. Regardless of how lofty the expectations were we always accomplished them as a unit.

Watching how this man worked and the things he was able to accomplish even though the resistance faced against him was awe-inspiring. It was not his job to lead our strength staff but I thought he had done one of the better jobs that I had seen from an associate director leading the staff. He would make sure we were organized for meetings, make sure everyone knew what their job was supposed to be and how to do their assigned task, he would talk to the boss for us about raises or taking care of the staff, he would fight for us for things we wanted and to put it metaphorically...he was our Jimmy Hoffa.

His leadership skills embodied a true servant leader. He never asked for anything even when you knew he needed it. He was always putting others first. So you might ask me, Don, if this type of leadership is so great how could one fail at being a servant? Well to illustrate the point of the importance of servant leadership, we must talk about its flaw...when it becomes worldly. And when it becomes worldly instead of staying true to its origins, it corrupts everything about it, bringing down the entirety of the population that has been influenced by it. I've watched this happen from afar and I've seen the devastation.

It's ironic to think that the only thing that ruins servant leadership is not being a servant. If you were a tyrant many things can bring you down; the people, your peers, the people you appointed into different roles, another country built on democracy and freedom. Any one of these other pieces could entirely wipe you off the face of the map. But if you're a servant leader, the only thing that can ruin you is you. Tyranny is built off of so many different things, such as fearmongering, power, greed, corruption, scandal, and all the other hateful things you can think of. But servant leadership is built off of one simple fact; your purpose is to serve others first. When you then turn to putting yourself first, the whole structure implodes from the inside out.

I knew a man whom I had consoled while he cried two times during my time in Georgia. This man was not only humble but holy in sorts. They eventually dubbed this man "The Statesboro Jesus". Now SJ, which I'll call him for short, was one of my early examples of what a servant looked like. He would always go out of his way to make sure others were taken care of first. He not only talked about servant leadership, but he embodied it. Often after practice, he would pick up the field the entire with the equipment staff. This is unheard of for a head coach at his level to do. I have never seen this done prior or since. Eventually based on the model he set I would help pick up the field with him. This went on for weeks the two of us, picking up the field after practice until eventually, more and more people started joining the cause.

On Christmas, I remember receiving not a Christmas bonus but a piece of mail with money in it from SJ. He didn't have to do this for all of us. But out of his salary, he gifted us all holiday cash. This may seem like a small thing to do for a man who was making a six-figure salary but I cannot stress to you how many coaches do not do that for their staff. Everything SJ did for us that the first year was uncommon and the results of that uncomanality was a very uncommon season. The year prior that same team had a 2-10 record. Our first year altogether with almost an entirely new staff, we went 10-3 with one of the only other bowl wins in school history. I witnessed all this and decided from that point on servant leadership was not only effective but the right way to lead a group of people. And then fall happened.

As we discussed earlier, only a servant's inability to serve will destroy the servant leadership model. What happened next is a clear example of that. The worst thing that could've happened after the 10-3 season was the fame that came in a small town after going 10-3. We all walked around like local heroes and were unfortunately treated as such. The nickname "Statesboro Jesus" came about, and the humble servant became the false idol. Servanthood is about the people, but idolization is about nothing more than the person themselves. When the leader becomes the idol, they shut off their ability to look outward through a lens of servanthood and instead think they deserve to be served. Many leaders today start this way and are successful for a time with certain populations. But I ask you, what is the price of one's soul?

Yes, you can sit there and say "Don, not every leader is a servant and they do just fine". And I would be forced to agree with you to the extent of things still get done. But then I would ponder if they got done because of or despite of the leader? I would also wonder what a day in that office looks like. I would wonder how happy those within the organization are or better yet how inspired are those people to come to work and make a perspective difference. And then you would say... probably very few if any. If you want to change the world you have to be different then the world.

There is no inspiration in imitation the inspiration is in originality. Servanthood is an original idea that goes against the grain of the very nature that inhabits the human body. That is why in 13+ years in the American workforce I have seen very few sustained examples of it. I'm not perfect but I am dependent on this model because I do not enjoy the type of leader, I have been before the servanthood model. Vain, arrogant, shallow, and prideful. All about myself and trying to make my name bigger. I had to eventually let all of that go to arrive at the point in the journey I'm at.

Part 2: Letting Go

I often say, "Jesus washed a man's feet but you can't (insert the task not being done)". I usually say in a joking tone but the reality behind it is very serious. We talked about the problems of modern leadership and what servanthood is. The next lesson I learned on my path in the quest to be a true servant leader was another important and valuable part of my journey. The lesson I learned was that if I wanted to be a great leader I would have to let go of every materialistic or idealistic thing I held so dear (in a sense). I had to shed the old and let the new be born because the old was self-serving and not the make-up of serving the people. The old was a man of the people in his mind but his actions did not follow. I had to learn to malt away to progress forward.

It's funny how life works. Since I started writing this book my life has drastically changed. It's also awesome and shocking to see how other people's lives have changed around. Most people during this stretch of the year in college athletics move on to new and better jobs due to so much turnover, firing, and hiring that happens in the winter months. It is currently January 9, 2022, to provide context for you that aren't in athletics or don't understand why we madmen do this (and madwomen as well). Though I find women to be a thousand times smarter and work through processes while we "adventure-seeking" men just jump job to job. Another of a long line of points to the ladies.

As the job market continues to change and people continue to move around in my industry you occasionally (unfortunately more often than not) see a puzzling move. For example, I've seen some people go from the trademark example of anti-servant to a more defined and upgraded leadership role. I don't throw stones from above the wall, my house is made from glass. I hope that they can go on to become the leaders that are needed to lead an organization and make the change. But how often do we see people move forward from mud to muck? Far too often unless something happens, change in those people does not occur. There is no malting process because they do not believe one needs to occur. I have been there myself. I did not malt when I didn't think I needed to. Why change who I am, what I believe, or my processes when they keep moving me forward? That would be a waste of time, right?

Wrong. We sure always continuously work on the malting process. The malt is what made us who we currently are, and the malt will continue to push us forward through our evolution as servant leaders. It would be asinine to think that after years of commercialism and capitalistic, money-hungry bs we've been spewed since we were old enough to remember that just one malt would suffice, and we magically come out on the other side "renewed". That would be like putting a bandage on a bullet wound and thinking "this should be fine". The malting is a continual lifelong process that one can assume gets easier over time because there is less to shed but more to maintain.

The malting process is all about getting rid of the bad qualities that hold you separate from being a true servant. For me were many but I am starting to hit the point in my malting seasons where the hard part for me is maintaining the good vs erasing the bad. I believe this is part of sustainability that happens when one gets to that tipping point between success and a one-time success. My first malt was a successful one. The first time I let go it was due to circumstances. I was tired of being so angry and so hateful, so I let go of the anger and hate I had for my current boss in Georgia. This allowed me to be at peace with my situation and freer-minded. It was what it was now let me work through it was my new mindset.

My second malt was a tad bit bigger as I had been saved and converted my life to Christianity. I under-emphasize bigger, this was a huge moment in my life. But in my extreme, young Christian self, I malted more than I could chew. I threw out every single thing that I did not want anymore. This wasn't a bad practice, but I had not been prepared for the execution that would need to take place. You see when you get rid of old habits you must replace those habits with something. I find the best way to do this is through having a plan of attack and slow checkpoints of execution. I want to do A but to get to A I will need to do B, C, D, E, F, and G. Once I have mastered every letter leading up I am ready to no longer be where I was at months or years ago. And I won't ever go back to what I was because I've forgotten who that person even was to go back to.

For me, I skipped the process in my second malt and some of my lesser desirables came screaming back. I had expelled the demons (bad leadership traits) but forgot to shut the window. Some of the demons realized the front door was locked, turned around defeated, and left. But others noticed the window was open and happily climbed right on in. It would take a year of strict meditation and conscious effort to get me back to level. This malt wasn't as tough as the others, but it was a slow-cooked one.

There have been other malts throughout my many seasons and sometimes you don't even know you're malting till you look back years later and reflect. I have had to let go of a lot of things during my times as a leader. I've been a director three times now and I have been a better version of myself every single time. Serving someone else is extremely hard and putting others first for the right reasons is also very hard. That's why your process in becoming better HAS to be a very hard, challenging process because if it's not then you won't complete it to its fullest.

Ego, pride, and almost anything self-fulfilling must be cast to the side if you want to be a true servant except for love. Love is a very self-fulfilling thing but also a very selfless thing. To me, love is a conundrum but whatever you do as a leader if it's with a heart of love usually you're in the right headspace and moving in the right direction. We can all agree on it then, keep love. And when I say cast out, I don't mean for the sake of "looking good" I mean to cast out with a plan of execution to make your organization and the people around you better by making yourself a better servant. There is no room for these undesirable traits on the path that we are going down.

Once, out of love, I took a 15-20k pay cut to give the staff I hired the money I could. This wasn't something that sat well with everyone around me in the outside world but it was what I felt I needed to do as a servant of my people. Doing such a thing was not easy for me. I wasn't making $100,000. I was set to make 60-65k and took it down to 45-50k. It was what it was and I was able to survive and be just fine. More importantly, as a leader, when I talked about sacrifice and servanthood it didn't fall on deaf ears because I showed I was about what I said I was about.

I had a boss who one time scolded the staff on servanthood and how we needed to be more willing as a staff to step up and take care of small things around the building. The problem isn't what he said because as a staff I agreed. The problem was that he wasn't doing it himself. He would leave his weights from his workout out and then expect one of us to pick it up for him before the next group started. He would not help us set up (this changed towards the end of my time at this particular place) and he would not help us break down (this was pretty much the same the entire time). When he had pulled us into the office to talk about servanthood, I thought to myself "what a joke" and the staff echoed the same sentiments in their heads as well.

This is all because my boss had yet to start his malting process. He hadn't let go. Of what? I do not exactly know. I cannot claim to know the feeling of walking in another man's shoes nor can I claim to truly know anyone after a year no matter how much time I've spent with them. Therefore, I cannot make reasonable assumptions about why someone would act how they act. But from what I have seen is that when you demand something of yourself but not of others...you think what you're demanding is beneath you to do yourself. If there is anything beneath you that you're too prideful to do then servanthood has been lost on you and will be lost on those you are imploring.

Letting go and moving on is in essence the same thing in terms of your malt. When I was tired of the old me, I moved forward with my new self. I took the old me and pushed him off a cliff. Unfortunately for me, I didn't give enough separation because he was able to grab me by the ankle and drag me down over time. Now old me lives across the street and we have mutual respect for our perspective differences in life. I can see old me's house and it's a nice house but I enjoy my house a lot better. My house has everything I want in it, I know how to move around in it a lot better and well I paid for it and pay I truly did.

Coming out of college I was piss hot and full of vinegar but also very unsure of myself. Most of my self-worth came from statistics and playing football. When I no longer had either I did not know how to exactly operate in the world. And I also did not know myself by any stretch of the imagination. I had fake confidence that was hiding one embarrassingly scary thing: I was not confident at all. I was coming off a relationship that had shattered my entire existence and erased whatever real confidence I thought I had at the time. On top of that I was going into an industry I knew very little about number one of which that I knew extremely little about was how volatile and egotistical my industry is.

My first internship was fine because I was treated like a player, and I acted like a player. I took commands and didn't ask any questions. Everything worked out pretty well for me based on that. My next internship was the same way but with a twist. I had done so well during the internship that a graduate assistant position was created for me. This was a very, very small step into my downfall as a leader without even knowing it. I truly do believe hard work should be rewarded. What else is there? Whatever you work hard for you should eventually be able to achieve if realistic steps are taken to achieve the desired outcome and the work is put in. But the danger is under which terms you accept your reward and how you view the new outcome.

I accepted the graduate assistant spot like someone would a freaking Oscar. Prideful, boastful, and now I felt like one of Hollywood's big wigs. I still hadn't made it nor did I know much nor did I have any real coaching ability. I could outwork people and I had a natural gift to coach, but I hadn't learned truly how just yet. Eventually, skip ahead a few steps and I'm a head strength coach at a good school and we're winning games. In my mind I was on a parade that whole season, waving my hands and catching roses as I drove past the people who came to see me. Skip ahead another step and I'm back trying to do right as a leader but still, something is just missing. Then skip to right here and what's the story going to be about me now? Third time's the charm?

Kaizen is a word that has stuck with me throughout my process. It means "continual change for the good". In essence, it means to always look at what works and what doesn't work and continue to move the needle towards positive growth. That is exactly what the malting process is about. I was an arrogant, arrogant, shallow bastard as a person, and I was that was my first time as a leader. Check that, I was not a leader back then, I was a boss. Then I turned into a servant with some pieces throughout my malting process. Now I am on a more concise and better path than I have ever been, and I am right where I want to be in my process.

This by no means has been an easy process for me by any means. My whole life up until I was saved had been about me even if I think it not. I was always a good teammate, and I played a very sacrificial role in college. I was a nose tackle, and my job was to make sure the linebackers could do their job effectively. Sure, I cared about winning but I really just cared about my stats. In college, I just cared about my playing time versus in high school I cared about stats because playing time was fortunately always there for me. Though I was a team captain in high school I was by no means a leader. I was a cocky SOB, and every single person knew it.

I would walk around like most jocks like my stuff didn't stink. And this carried over later in my life. Like most, my bad habits started in high school and continued until adulthood. It also didn't help the fact that I am a master escape artist. I make Harry Houdini look like Mickey Mouse with my natural ability to walk right out of bad situations. As a former assistant once said, "you walk into s#$t and walk out shining". This is something I always took mild offense to as it implied that I never had a plan, that I just would willy nilly everything and goes through life without a thought process. The escape was always and is always planned to even the minors of details.

With all that being said we now focus our attention on you, the reader. You're probably sitting there wondering "when will we hear less of the self-pity and more of the self-help" and the answer is a resounding YOU WON'T. Only you can help yourself. There is nothing I can say or do that will help you unless you first decide to help yourself. Simply put, someone offering you a million dollars does nothing to change your life, realizing you need the money and accepting the money is what begins the start of the change. I can only offer you stories, self-tragedies, and advice. If you decide not to take this and make a conscious effort to change who you are as a leader for the betterment of your people, then that all falls to the wayside.

I don't do this often, but I am currently coming off an inconsistent moment. I try my hardest not to get too high and not to get too low but stay in the middle. I want to master all my feelings and stay consistent in my actions and my thoughts. That is one of the things that helped me change who I was into who I am. But currently, I have momentarily broken from my oath of consistency, I've realized this after a day of being too high up and now I am bringing myself back to the middle ground where I can focus and attack my goals with savage realism, not false optimism.

I say all that to say this, I realized who I was, I realize who I am, and I know who I want to be. And every day I must keep cutting the fat off the undesirables to be someone I look up to. I don't do this for myself because, in my arrogant past, I lusted for myself. I lusted everything about me and it was a world circled around serving me. Whether intentional or not, my actions were run by an unknown intentionality to serve myself out of the lust I had for myself. Now I have learned to love myself. And loving yourself isn't just loving the beautiful parts, it's knowing and being real about the ugly parts as well.

Loving yourself is about staying committed to what you are about no matter how hard it is to stay on the path. Through hardship, pain, and tears you still love yourself enough to be about what you said you were going to be about. And what I decided through Christ that I was going to be about was serving others, no matter what the personal costs I may lose are. Just so long as others can gain from the sacrifices I make for them, that's considered a life well lived to me.

Now we double back once again to where we left off twice before, you the reader. How do you let go? How do you stop holding onto everything? How do you lose yourself in order to become free? How do you get past all my questions and find the arbitrary answer? By having an unrelenting commitment to becoming better every single day even if it's only by 1%. 1% better every day leads to a 365% increase in productivity over the course of a year. Even if you go from 0 to 365 that's not too shabby.

But that one percent is hard to do because as easy as it sounds to get 1% better every day, the reverse can happen and you can get worse on any given day, and you will have bad days regardless of your level of commitment to self-improvement. Everyone has bad days, no one is perfect and accepting that fact is very important because it's very real. The difference I've found between people who make a real change (winners) and the ones who let life just go by the wayside (losers) is that winners are real. Winners have all the same problems as losers, but winners look at the problem as a challenge that can be overcome or used as a tool for self-improvement.

Taking everything that you have learned and done up to this point and analyzing it from the lens of a winner makes change much easier to digest. No one likes to change but it's inevitable. Change can lead to brilliance and breakthrough. The first step of improving oneself is to take everything and change it for the good. You have to look at what your makeup is. I don't mean the cliché checklist; I mean really sit down and dissect yourself in the mirror surgeon style. What makes you tick? What are your inner demons? Where do your wants come from? What are they fueled by? Are you a prick because your dad was a prick or are you a prick because no one showed you any respect growing up? These are all important questions to answer. Dive deep into the psyche.

You have toxic habits and toxic traits that are preventing you from reaching the next level of your development. It is important not to hate those things but embrace them, come face to face with them and then drive them out with an unrelenting effort. Toxicity makes you float but what I'm asking you to do is grab onto something that will pull you deep into the waters drowning not only your soon-to-be old self but the toxicity along with it. We don't need the old you if you want to improve, we need something better to reemerge from the depths of the water.

The me I had been my whole life is dead and gone. He tried to struggle, and I had to grab on to something heavier to make sure he didn't just sink but stayed sunk. Morbid as it sounds it is very real. Again, this book wasn't meant to be all sunshine and rainbows because the things I'm talking about doing are very hard to do. I'm not giving you a perfect picture to gaze at, I am telling you what the real path to being a servant looks like. I couldn't serve myself and others, therefore I had to get rid of who I was to be a better servant. Everything I do, what I am made of, is to serve others. I haven't taken pay cuts and unjust wages so I could thrive, I did it for others too. Now a days I is a very vague term. There is a me, but servanthood is much bigger than the person. And that is the sacrifice I have chosen to make to become the person that can be there for others, not out of a desire but out of love.

You see love fuels everything. A strong love fuels the urge to help others. A strong self-love fuels the urge to help yourself. To let go and move forward you are going to need both. If you're reading this book, you're one of three things; a relative, a friend, or in need of change. And maybe you're all three. I'm going to assume you picked up this book because you were drawn by the want to be a better leader which means there are traits that lie within you that are mucking up the path to greatness. Let them go. There is no reason to hold onto things that do not progress us forward in life.

Arrogance is not an elixir. Pride, arrogance, and contempt are like a $200 bottle of bourbon. It should be sipped on on special occasions not gargled down every single day. Use these emotions for what their useful purposes are but do not live in these zones. It's okay to be proud of a big accomplishment, It's ok to get pissed off for greatness, and It's okay to think you're the best at something to fuel your confidence when needed. These are all examples of a sip from the glass. But if you live your life based on these traits, they then become toxic and will lead you down a dark path as they once did for me. Letting go is literally taking the worse form of yourself and fixing it. You know how: with consistency and discipline. It's not easy but it is worth it.

At the end of the day, we should all want to be better. Life is about change and if that change isn't towards something better then what purpose is there to exist? Are you just here to be here or are you living life? And this isn't a get rich quick grandiose speech it is a very real question. I did not want to just continue taking up space on this planet, living in my corrupt selfishness. What I was called to do was to help others improve their lives. That is what being a servant is all about.

The world will call servants slaves or idealists. But once you delve deep into the process of changing yourself for the better than you will have a deep sense of relief. You will feel a sense of pride in the new you because it's going to be hard to accomplish these changes and stay consistent in them. And more so in a metaphorical sense, you will become an alien. I use the term alien because most of the world is okay with being average. You are choosing not to be. And those who do try to better themselves usually do as a form of later self-fulfillment. You on the other hand are choosing to better yourself so that you can serve others. This concept will seem alien to others and more than likely make others uncomfortable around you which is understandable and completely okay.

Show them the way. Lead them down the path of personal enlightenment. Try your hardest and never give up or give in. The hardest battle is between you and you. Once this battle is fought everything else is rehearsal. Never forget why you started this path. There are people that I have served that have turned against me. These same people have betrayed me in the deepest sense of the word. I still help them. I still extend a hand when needed. I do not forget but I forgive because it's not about me. I am a servant of the people and I have to remind myself no one is perfect and I truly don't believe we were made to be. I'm no better than anyone else so who am I to judge. If they are willing to accept help when needed, then I am more than willing to give it.

I say all this because there was a time in my arrogance that someone didn't give up on me. I had gotten into a scuffle with a former boss as he transitioned to a new role. He had offered me a chance to come with him, but I arrogantly turned it down. This man still reaches out to me today and helps me even when I don't ask for it. He always looks out for me and takes interest in my life and what I am doing in my career. I haven't worked for him in over six years and he owes me nothing. He is training athletes at the highest level and has a family of his own. He's a devote father and husband and to me, he is a devote leader. I owe this man everything and have given him little to nothing. Yet he still finds time to try and help me. If this man can commit to serving, then there is no reason we all can't.

Part 3: Servanthood

There is a man named Donald Day, but this name and this person have a very vague meaning. There is a title I possess called Director, but this term has a very vague meaning. The truest definition of who I am is a servant. That is the term that can best describe not only myself as a person but define the role I currently inhabit. If it were HR okay, I would change my title from Director of Strength and Conditioning to Servant Leader. That is a title that more accurately describes who I am and what I do in my role and my roles prior.

Whether you are an assistant, director, manager, CEO, or whatever title was given to you we all can be servant leaders. Being a servant is a calling to do work for other people not in your best interest but theirs. This goes above and beyond any title given by the HR people (all due respect to those in HR). People sometimes say "sacrificial leader" but in my eyes, this makes a martyr out of the term. Which emphasizes the person and not the people. To serve is to sacrifice so this term "sacrificial leader" is redundant, it should be understood in the job description. The term was told to me once by a man who did no such sacrifices and was an oppressive force if I've ever seen one. Therefore, I have chosen to let that go by the wayside.

Not to sound too melodramatic but reaching the point of true servanthood is similar to reaching the point of enlightenment. As stated before being a servant is alien to most people as it had been to me prior. Pride mixed servanthood with slavery and there is a big difference between the two. Alfred wasn't Batman's slave, he served Batman even so far as to sacrifice his life on many different occasions (rebirth in comic books occurs often). I'm not advocating sacrificing your life that seems a tad dramatic and it's not a comic book, but some have ie MLK or Malcolm X for the cause of serving others. To those people, I give my ultimate respect.

In terms of servant leadership, what does that look like? It means that you are walking alongside those who have entrusted you to lead them. You're their leader and they will all be looking at you either through admiration or disgust based on your actions with the group as a whole and an individual basis. And don't for a second think that just because the overall group is happy that the individuals are all on the team. There are deeper leadership lessons outside the scope of this book but for right now we'll address leadership through the eyes of the servant.

A leader serves both the group and the individuals. Both must be served at a high level and usually, it's the individuals that make up the group that attention should be paid the most. The same as one leak can sink a ship, one unhappy employee can cause strain to the group. And just because the group is performing at a high level this does not mean they are getting the service they need. High performance is the bottom standard. The low-hanging fruit of being a "director" or "GM" is that you acquired that position because your efforts result in high-level production (hopefully). Therefore, this is an expectation, not a bargaining tool used to gain meaningful relationships with employees.

In two separate instances, I had a high-performing staff (staff A and B). Staff A admittedly functioned at a higher level and performed better than staff B but regardless both were high-performing groups. A member of staff A (we'll say Sheron) came to my employment for career development. One staff B (we'll nickname her Suzie) came to my employment to learn from me. Sheron was very pleased with how her job was done and she performed at a high level yet was discontent, spewing negativity. Suzie wasn't so sure of herself and felt as if she needed more reassurance and guidance yet did not spew discontent.

Sheron and I had many sit-downs that often ended in tears and hugs. We worked together and fixed things that I saw with her style of work and her style of being an employee. At the end of the day, Sheron and I would never have dinner together, but we were able to work through difficulties and differences to make sure she was a high-functioning member of the team and not one that was poking holes in the boat as we sailed out. Suzie (part of staff B) and I sat down to talk on many occasions. I had neglected as a leader how much she needed to be led. I took for granted the fact that staff A could function without as much instruction as staff B needed. This is not to say staff B was worse or incapable they needed from me what I had been put in front of them to do: service.

Suzie and I discussed many of the things that I had overlooked as a leader and as a servant. I discussed things she needed to work on as well. In the end, Suzie and I still communicate and are helpful peers now that we no longer work for the same company. Both Sheron and Suzie have gone on to do great things in this profession. Suzie became a director and Sheron moved on to the same role in a larger company. Though I never saw eye to eye with Sheron, I'm still proud of the conscious efforts she made to better herself and in that same token better how I did things as well.

These are two examples of taking care of individuals while taking care of the group regardless of how highly functional the team performs. As a servant, you MUST serve each individual member of the team regardless of how the level of performance. Especially if the collective performs at a high level because this is often when the individuals get overlooked. As stated in the examples I have gone under the assumption that the individuals are fine if the collectives are performing at a high level and this clearly was not the case. On the same token servitude has to be individualized. What help Sheron excel was not the same as what helped Suzie. This seems obvious to some but to most, it can be a point that is easily missed as in my abysmal way.

We talk about continual change in part 2 of the book and somehow in part 3 improving gets brought up again. Why? Because this is a constant reality in your drive as a servant leader. The goal is to be better every day for those whom you lead. Those two situations weren't situations that happened to me decades ago...they were within two or three years of this current moment. I didn't beat myself down or think of myself as a failure because of a misstep I used those missteps to step correct into my next step. Often when people judge someone as a failure it is because they need the security of you failing to rationalize something missing in themselves. Never forget that point either.

Servanthood is tough. A pastor once told me "being a Christian is committing to a lifetime of suffering, it is not easy". There are no sunshine and rainbows for those who try to walk the path of Jesus in this life, I do not believe. That may be misguided but in my eyes, that's how I see it. We are dependent on Jesus to guide our steps and we are trying to be separate from a world that wants us all to indulge in the things that separate us from our journey. The joy is in following the one who gave us this life and helping others along the way, eventually leading to our meeting with our savior. My take on Christianity is not much different than my take on being a servant leader.

To commit to a lifetime of servanthood with no want of gain seems like committing to a lifetime of defaulting on any future profit. It seems like you are giving up wants and desires for nothing. Like you are committing to a lifetime of suffering just for the benefit of others. And in some ways at this point of my journey maybe I am and maybe we are, but it is worth it. Along the way, we are helping others grow and prosper and continue to help others grow and prosper. We may be the sacrifice that starts a change of empowerment for the rest of the world. Someone must be crazy enough to dare to do it and why not us?

The assistant who stole my ideas and made them his own is doing wonders for himself. He's building his brand and helping others in their lives. He is creating a better world for those around him including his girlfriend and his family. At the end of the day regardless of how it happened or how it may have hurt me, isn't that what my purpose of serving others is about? It's about helping people regardless of self and in this instance, that's what ended up happening. I may not appreciate the way that it happened, but the results are that man is in a better situation and now putting others in better situations inadvertently due to my service to him. Again, servanthood is committing to a lifetime of suffering for the betterment of other people and that is one testament to it.

Many people have used my name to prosper in this industry yet stabbed me in the back at some point in time. That too is okay. I reference Jesus in this book and follow his entire model as a way of life, yet I sin every single day. Holding on to negative emotions takes you away from the ability to serve others. Sheron is not and was not someone I particularly liked and for all intents and purposes was not a good person. And it took me a while to be a better leader for her because I had discontent in my heart but once I let that go and was able to converse without anger. I was able to serve her better.

Suzie had stabbed me in the back blatantly. And I was hateful because of it. I let that hate go and went on to later in life recommend her for a high-level job. At the time I fought through spite and tried to help her to the best of my ability. Fortunately, we are still in good standing, and she has gone on to do good things not only in her career but in life. There is a Donald Day but that is a vague term of who I am, I am a servant.

When you begin to serve others, it will be frustrating, discouraging, awesome, tiresome, and all the above. You cannot give in to the doubt of "am I doing things the right way". For every person who I've lost, I have gained fifty more. Even those who initially wandered away came back and with open arms, I have always accepted them. There will be times when someone who is genuinely caring for others wellbeing will unsettle some. They won't exactly know how to take you or the genuine nature of servanthood. That's okay. Slow cook everything, don't just throw servanthood down someone's throat. You have to feed a baby milk not chicken wings and that's the same to some people with a servant leader mentality.

It is not a style of leadership where you do everything and they reap the benefits. The style of leadership I'm talking about is giving your all to someone so they feel empowered to lead themselves. Eventually, all you're there for is to serve as a guiding light. The values instilled will be the road to the path they walk. All "credit" goes to the collective of student and teacher due to the simple fact that you are walking alongside each other not one in front of the other. Even the word credit is a rudimentary term as the only real reward is seeing your followers go forth and prosper making many more disciples of the discipline you have shown.

In no way, shape or form does this mean you have to be a Jesus figure. That would be counterintuitive making yourself an ideal but following the ideologies of Jesus. I'm far from anything that resembles Jesus safe to say for the fact that I know I must be dependent on him to live the life I've been called to lead. As a servant, don't pose as an all-seeing, perfect ideal because you are not. That road leads to a dark path and opens up the doors for negative emotional connections to rush in. All you are is a person who was put into a leadership role that is trying to do better than most that are called to lead.

Servanthood is not sexy but it's the road that leads to the ultimate empowerment of your people. My mother often told me that people don't change and more often than not that is true. But what people love to do is follow. This is a fact we all know. Whether it be the latest trends, the newest ideologies, or the run of the mill following the crowd. As a human race sometimes I think we were born with a percentage of us chosen to lead and others chosen to follow. But even at some level, the leaders are just more charismatic or brave or tenacious followers who are following a calling that inspired them to step up to the plate.

We follow because leading is scary. As a leader, you have made yourself the ultimate target and put yourself out there for criticism and critique by all who have eyes to see. But you must not be scared as leading is a higher calling, not something that every person in the world may understand. All of your decisions won't make everybody happy but if they come from the right heart then there is no need to worry about what pleases some and displeases others, the best choice is the right choice.

On the opposite side of fear comes bravery. There is no one braver than the person who forsakes all personal gain for the cause of empowering others. There is truly nothing to fear once you have faced your inner demons and written off the prized possessions the world says you want but don't necessarily need. Servant leaders do not worry about what is right for them, they are too busy thinking of the collective. There is no time to be scared, the only thing you have time to focus on is leading those around you and empowering them every single day.

Outside of service, empowerment is the top tool of a servant leader. Empowerment can come in many different forms but by definition, empowerment is the uplifting of others to accomplish their goals. Everyone has their own specific individual goals bred from a specific set of circumstances. Again, why you need to lead the individual as well as the group. Empowerment done right can lend itself to miraculous breakthroughs within your group of followers. I have seen many empowered people defy obstacles that most would consider roadblocks. I too have been empowered to do things that I never imagined were possible for me. If empowerment was sold in pill form it would be banned within a week.

Empowerment and servanthood aren't just feel-good give-aways with no hard work to be earned. I don't go around like a flower girl throwing these things around carelessly and free-spirited. They are things that are hard roads ahead. Empowerment in itself is a miraculous thing but to be empowered is only the start. I was empowered to fight against racial injustices that I saw at a former institution but that was just the beginning. The path after that was paved with hardships but I was prepared to face them because I was empowered to do so. Just like receiving service. It's not something that I let people take for granted. If I am going to serve you, there must be a hard nose dive into what it is I'm trying to help you accomplish. That usually starts with a lot of hard conversations and a lot of self-reflection.

I have always been brought up to work like you are at a higher level than what your title says. If I'm a graduate assistant, I'm working like I'm the head strength coach and so on and so forth. I empower all my followers to do the same. I tell them "do not work like assistants, see the world through the lens of the seat above you". I empower them to be the best version of themselves and shoot for the stars (cliché sorry but not sorry). With that, I can't just rant like a propaganda-driven leader, showing them no way of actually achieving their goals. I serve them in their quest to be their best selves.

This is different for every person. But the base level part of this is taking away anything that would prevent them from succeeding. If money is an issue, I'll find a way to make it a non-issue. If time commitment is going to be a cause of stress or burnout, then I will handle some of the heavy load until they are at the point they can shoulder it themselves. If development is needed, then I will drop whatever I need to to make sure they are getting the development they need.

I don't want any excuses for why they are not able to succeed or anything to drag them down from succeeding. In that same token though my expectation is they move forward with great relentlessness in their process of accomplishment whatever that process looks like. And again, for different people based on different goals, these processes will look different. But if I am empowering you and serving you to be a CEO (something that we had previously discussed was a goal of yours) then I shouldn't have to stay on you to get to work on time. Or I shouldn't have to continually remind you of the commitment level it is going to take to get there.

There is a lofty idea of what servanthood is not and there is a realism to what it is. I was once told that being a Christian isn't about perfection and that God does not expect that from you. It was stated to me that being a Christian is about dependence on a path set out fourth for you by the creator and believing he sent his one son down to die for your salvation which makes you already saved no matter what you do so fourth as you believe those things. But at no point did I think "okay cool now I can do absolutely anything that I want". In the most watered-down sense of the word, this is breaking the bro code for sure.

And outside of the legal ramifications that would come from doing anything I wanted whenever I wanted, this simply is not the life that I have committed to living. If I have decided on committing to a life of self-reflection and continual improvement with a dependency on values then why would I go against that regardless of how much God loves me? It's something I cannot rationalize. As stated earlier sin is separation and I try every day to be better but I don't use imperfection as a get out of jail free card for my sins.

In the same token if someone is trying to give everything, they have to you then why wouldn't you want to continue to help yourself. All that I ask of my followers is that they help themselves. I'm not asking them to convert to a religion or make me an ideal in any way shape or form. I ask the people that I have been called to lead to look in the mirror and find ways of self-improvement and I will be by their side the entire time. As a servant all I want to do is help people through empowerment and service. And that is all real servant leadership is when you get to the brass tax: empowerment and service.

I stated earlier this is not an easy path for the leader or the follower. This is not a normal form of leadership. It almost at first seems soft which is something most can't stomach. That isn't softness it's a vulnerability which if you're going to lead you have to have. You are choosing to give people the ultimate access to you without hiding behind a wall of toughness and false pretenses. But remember you're not their friend, you're their leader. Friends have a habit of sometimes telling their friends what they want to hear, not what they need to hear. A leader will break you down from top to bottom to help you become better. And you will be better for doing the latter to your followers, I promise you that.

It's not easy to in essence sit down with someone and say "I love you but you have terrible traits so let's sit down and do some self-reflection and in my complete transparency will help you through some of our similar bad traits that I've worked or been working on". It's not easy but it's worth it. And during these moments of reflection, it's often can be used as a personal check-up into how you've been handling dealing with your demons to see if they're still in check or do you need realignment again yourself.

There are a lot of Christian undertones (or maybe just blatant tones) in this chapter and throughout this book. This is something I am not oblivious to by any means. I was in Sally's beauty shop yesterday buying beard oil and having a conversation with the general manager. They asked me what brought me to Kentucky, and I said "work". They then asked what I do and I said "I am an author writing a book called The Servant about servant leadership" and they responded, "Oh is that a Christian book?". I am not a pastor nor am I a painted image of a Christian. My whole philosophy derives from Jesus's model so that is why the references are just the same as those who reference

Alexander the Great when it comes to Stoicism. I don't believe I'm a great example of a Christian, but I am one none the less and that is a fact I do not hide, just as I would not hide the fact of being a proud black man.

Regardless of your belief system, I think that to be a good servant leader you need to remember the principles of where this system of leadership was developed. Just as when I read a stoic quote and commit it to my head the same you should do with servanthood. There are going to be times when followers disappoint and times when you want to get frustrated but forgive and stay patient. Remember this: the woman searches harder for the coin she lost than the 10 that are in her possession.

Pouring your all and leaving yourself so vulnerable to your followers will eventually at some point or the other lead to heartbreak. I remember my first heartbreak. I gave my all to a group of followers and they maliciously betrayed me. One was a person who had jealousy, one was a person who had a cunning to themselves, one was one with a high degree of selfishness and the other one would sway in the wind. Now I must say the other two on that staff that I didn't describe were loyal people and chose not to be involved in the setup and warned me about what was happening but by that time it had already happened.

After the four horsemen went to betray me, I met with each of them one on one. One lied and pretended to be a friend trying to help me better myself. One hugged me and apologized for the misunderstanding. One was cold and callous as always. And the other started to bawl their eyes out in front of me apologizing for the misunderstanding and not knowing what was going on in my own private life. I find sometimes when you leave yourself vulnerable there will be people who see it as an opportunity to seize "what's you have" but the ironic part of it was I was not sitting on a throne. I was standing right beside all of them.

If it hadn't been for my vocal nature against sexism, racism and all other forms of ism's I experienced in my last few months with that particular company, then the lies spread by my assistants would have been the last straw for me. I could fight the battles on the outside but realizing I had lost the collective broke my heart. When I gave my two weeks it's funny...one of the horsemen called me a coward. I loved them through it anyway. One of the horsemen tried to recant their lies but by then it simply did not matter and I loved them through it the same. As hard as it was for me, I still loved them through it.

Those were the worst moments of my life. One of the horsemen blatantly took everything I had built and changed it to better suit themselves while I was still there while claiming to be someone who wanted the best for me. The other horsemen were receiving career opportunities based on things I had previously sacrificed to get them those opportunities. Meanwhile, I was watching a castle I had built brick by brick being torn down by those who I had loved and trusted to build with me. Being a servant, just as being a Christian, is committing to a life of suffering.

And in all those horrible moments, those horrible months, there were bright spots. I had athletes being coached by the horsemen who would want to take me to lunch or have dinner with me and say they saw what was happening but stood by my side. This was one of the biggest compliments I could have received. Not because I had people with me to make me feel better but because I had at some level empowered my athletes enough to be able to see with their own eyes. And on my staff were two of my former athletes. Both of which never left my side. Who have gone on to do great things. I love those two members of staff B.

The hatred did not just stop when I walked away. There seemed to be those out in the industry that had been waiting for a moment to strike. I had people that called me for help when they were starting in their careers now trying to make sure I would never get another job. I had a man who slept on my couch spread false rumors and destroy connections I had. At that point in time, I was so hurt and so lost and had no idea what I was going to do. I had nothing to grab on to and no hope for myself. I had given my all to everyone, I had left myself completely vulnerable and the rats had feasted, leaving me with nothing left.

But one day at the SEC championship game that I was attending about a month later a former athlete that I had just been coaching approached me. She had respected me enough to recommend me for a position. That recommendation led to an offer. That offer led to me getting back on my feet again and making great connections at the job that I was at. That job led me back to a director title that I currently have now. None of that would have been possible with the service and the empowerment that I poured into every single person around me regardless of how vulnerable it left me.

In the darkness that will happen, you must always strive to find the light. I never said this was going to be easy or that it would have a happy ending. My happy ending could very much so be a completely different ending. And my story is not over yet. I don't know when the vulnerability will lead to me getting hurt again (like in Georgia) but if I can positively impact the lives of even one or two people then it was all worth it for me. If I can empower a person that was shaky coaching five people to go on to be a women's basketball director then I have done my job. And if I can serve an athlete who tore a pec before the season to go on and become a Super Bowl champion then I have done my job.

Servanthood isn't cookie-cutter, but it is simple. It is giving up your all for someone else to get their all. It is having real conversations to move people forward. It is sacrificing not to be a martyr but to be a light in someone's life. It is suffering for a purpose, their purpose. It's realizing that the person that is you is a very vague object, you now lie within the service of the people. The people are you and you are the people. Let the joy you find be found in the people's success. Let the pride you gave up be regifted in seeing others go on to do great things because of your empowering ways.

I hope the people you impact going forward share this dream and de-sire to change the corrupt way leadership has become. No more of a boss-centered approach but an approach centered around the better-ment of the people. I hope that when you put this book down you are driven into a deep dive of self-reflection for the improvement of oth-ers' lives. I hope you go out and lead with a burning passion to make the people around you better. And at the end of your career or time on this earth, I hope the people remember you for who you are and al-ways what you stood for. And that isn't as (insert name) because that is a very vague term. I hope they remember you as a servant leader who served with glorious purpose.

Epilogue: The Beginning

I will not lie to you...I thought of MLK Jr. giving a speech the whole time I was writing that last paragraph. The spirit of the Black Panthers of times past rose from their graves and possessed my body for that part and I thank them for it. I've never written an epilogue before, but I have read quite a few and the thing that always bothers me is...I never really want to read them. Why not just make another chapter if I'm going to be forced to read this long-drawn-out ending to the book? I find, personally, that I enjoy most the books that just end. But I had an epilogue in mind, and you paid for this epilogue so an epilogue you shall receive.

I think the end of the journey to servanthood is not the end but the beginning. Just the same as this book. I didn't write this book to explain the ending of servant leadership. I wrote it so that you can go on to serve others. That is a lifelong task and does not end until your very last breath on this earth has been taken. Even when I'm on my death bed, I'll probably ask the doctor if he needs help with anything before I leave this mortal coil.

It's important to remember something I did not talk about too much in-depth. Recharging and servicing your loved ones. I do not do a great job at this by any means. But I can tell you what I'm trying to accomplish and how I'm trying to get better to aid you if you struggle with these two things. I hope that you are further ahead in your development in these two areas than I am but if not then here are some actual "self-help" type things that you can decide to use or not.

Servicing your loved ones is something that I struggle with. I don't know if my upbringing has made me emotionally frozen when it comes to family or not. Everyone has a flaw and my flaw is though I love my family dearly, I find it hard to express that love the way I want consistently. I'm not a ghost or anything like that in terms of my connection with my family but as I grow older, I realize I need to do more. That is part of the reason I moved from Arizona to Kentucky. One to start a family and two to be by my family. The time zone difference hurt my ability to communicate with my family especially my older family members. This was something that weighed on me heavily as none of us have figured out how to get any younger.

Being in Arizona was also hurting my ability to start a family and give the time commitment to my future children that I would want to give to them. I will not be an absentee father and I felt if I stayed in Arizona I would be. That was not acceptable to me. I realized my job, though fulfilling my purpose, was also selfish the way I went about things career-wise. I have moved my wife around the country and hadn't let her pursue her goals, I also was causing us not to be in a stable enough situation to have children. These two things were unacceptable once I realized it through our conversations and deep reflection. I had to make a change.

I may not be a Power 5 strength coach anymore, but I am still a strength coach making an impact on a high number of athletes at a division 1 level. The logo was pride, the function of who I am is supposed to be devoid of that so I devoided it. I can now give my time to my future children, my family, and my wife. This was a necessary move for my life and in no way, shape or form is something that should be seen as a sacrifice. It was a necessity not a sacrifice.

As with my family though I do get drained at work, talking to them helps refuel me. I am making time to reach out and talk to them even if it's for five minutes. Again, not a sacrifice it is a necessity. As I have chosen to be the best husband I can be, I have equally chosen to be the best son. Our families couldn't visit us at any time in Arizona like they now can in Kentucky which is only seven hours away from our hometowns of Cleveland and Akron (Akron being far superior).

The recharge is the part I'm still working on. I haven't been very successful in most years but I'm still trying to grasp this concept. You can't fill someone else's cup if your cup is empty. Though at times I feel selfish taking time for myself, I also feel unfulfilled if I don't have the energy to give to others. The selfish thing would be to think that I am always needed. I'm not. I'm just a guy. Thinking that you are more than a person is prideful. I serve so I need to make sure I can give service and not just a quick fix. I have felt burnout before, and it is very real. Stress can build up and blow up out of nowhere.

One time, after the passing of an athlete, I broke down crying in front of my volleyball team. It was an emotional and amazing moment for all involved. We hugged and comforted each other as a collective of people who had just faced tragedy and loss. Though for me...I had faced nothing. I did not know at the time, but I was not crying because of the loss of an athlete. I never knew this athlete, nor had I ever met him. I was crying because his death opened the flood gates of some deep-rooted stress I had been ignoring.

The sad part is that I did not even realize this until it was pointed out to me months later. Yes, the loss of anyone is tragic but I did not know that athlete any more than I had known Kobe Bryant or Betty White. This was a red flag for me. I needed to find ways to recharge myself otherwise I was going to run myself straight into the ground. So how did I do that? I delved into my psyche and found out what brings me light.

There are certain people I know I need to talk to at least once a week that are my energy givers. My wife, my family, and my friends are all energy givers. One friend, who is now an assistant athletic director, speaks the language that is Don Day. She gives me light and like any good friend tells me the real and does not allow me to wallow in self-pity. The times where she has caught me doing that, she straightens me out right away.

For six months I was on a self-pity tirade. We talked and I was looking for more pity to add to my pot. What she did was the exact opposite. She told me the source of my problems came from the fact that I did not love myself. I didn't want to hear this, but it was what I needed. This tidbit of information helped me realign and get back on track. For all her brashness and harsh ways, I love her to death for helping me realign when I need it.

I enjoy a glass of bourbon, a strong cigar, and video games. Video games are a nightly routine for me just lifting is a weekly routine for me. On top of that, I need a sharp mind, so I force myself to get adequate amounts of sleep. Though I feel like sleep is a waste of time, I find ways to get 5-8 hours a night. This is progress to my normal 4-5 hours a night that I used to run on. I also make sure to try and take care of my body both physically through lifting and mentally through reflection and nutrition.

These are all ways I have found to mitigate stress and manage the heavy toll servanthood can have on a person. Though I am following Jesus's model, I must remind myself that I am not Jesus. I'm sure at some point even he got tired. And if he got tired then it's understandable that I will get exhausted in following. I need to make sure I am at my best so that I can constantly give my best. I am serving others, so I need to be able to serve fully not at a part-time two-star rating.

There it is. The end of the book but the lessons spoken about must not be a one-time reading. You must constantly self-reflect and self-check-in order to move forward. Continual change for the good is not just for those you serve but also for you as well. Lacking the ability to take care of your health is a toxic trait that must be addressed if you want to be an effective leader. Never forgot that. But always remember that taking care of yourself (setting boundaries) is not just for you but for the people. If your heart is for the people, then where your heart leads is always going to be the right place. Go forth and prosper not with a whisper but with relentless determination fueled by a glorious purpose.